Fish & Seafood

COOKBOOK

ideals®

Ideals Publishing Corporation
Nashville, Tennessee

CONTENTS

This book is one of a series of cookbooks including the following titles:

Budget Saving Meals Cookbook
Chicken and Poultry Cookbook
Grill and Barbecue Cooking
Ground Meat Cookbook
Guide to Microwave Cookbook
Hershey's Chocolate and Cocoa Cookbook
Low Calorie Cookbook
Lunch and Brunch Cookbook
Old-Fashioned Family Cookbook
Soup, Salad and Sandwich Cookbook
Quick & Simple Cooking for Two

30-Minute Meals Cookbook
All Holidays Menus Cookbook
American Regional Cookbook
Boys & Girls Cookbook
Christmas Cookbook
Country Baking Cookbook
Fish and Seafood Cookbook
Light & Delicious Cookbook
Casseroles & One Dish Meals
New Salad Cookbook
Wok Cookbook

These and other Ideals books are available in a SOFTCOVER edition in bulk quantities at quantity discount for fund-raising or premium use. For information, please write SPECIAL SALES DEPARTMENT, Ideals Publishing Corporation, P.O. Box 140300, Nashville, TN 37214

The HARDCOVER edition of selected Titles is published in a limited edition for the exclusive use of Wayne Matthews Corporation, P.O. Box 54, Safety Harbor, FL 34695.

Published by Ideals Publishing Corporation
Nashville, Tennessee

FISH AND SHELLFISH BASICS

For centuries people have looked to the sea for one of their primary sources of protein. They have broiled, boiled, baked, and barbecued both fish and shellfish for every meal and every occasion. Today, with renewed interest in low-fat, high-nutrition, natural foods, we once again acknowledge the importance of fish in our diets.

Fish is both healthful and delicious. It is a natural source of high-quality protein, yet contains considerably less fat than meat. Furthermore, fish provides every bit as much variety as meat. There is a type and texture to suit virtually every taste and budget.

Fat and Lean Fish

While we might not think of fat on fish in the same terms as we think of fat on meat, fish does contain a certain amount of fat. There is, in fact, a direct relationship between the taste and texture of a species of fish and its fat content.

Fish with high fat content are usually stronger in flavor and tend to have darker flesh than lean fish. Because they will remain moist when cooked at high temperatures, fat fish are ideal for baking, broiling, barbecuing, or grilling. Lean fish, on the other hand, are drier. Rather than fatty oil distributed throughout the flesh, the fat of a lean fish is concentrated in the liver. Since the liver is discarded when the fish is cleaned, most of the fat content is removed before cooking or eating. Lean fish tend to dry out too much when cooked at high temperatures and are usually more palatable when prepared in a style that involves a basting process. Steaming and poaching lean fish are excellent methods of preparation, as they replenish much of the moisture normally lost in cooking.

Fat Fish: Albacore, Bluefish, Herring, Lake Trout, Mackerel, Pompano, Rainbow Trout, Salmon, Sardines, Sturgeon, Tuna, and Whitefish.

Lean Fish: Carp, Catfish, Cod, Flounder, Haddock, Halibut, Pike, Pollock, Red Snapper, Sea Bass, Smelt, Sole, Swordfish, Yellow Perch, and Turbot.

Cooking the Fish

It is important to remember that, whether fat or lean, broiled or poached, fish never should be overcooked. When it comes to fish, there are no such things as rare, medium, and well-done.

To determine the proper amount of cooking time, follow this general rule devised by the Canadian Department of Fisheries: Measure the thickest part of the fish, then cook the fish for approximately 10 minutes per inch. In other words, a fish that measures 3 inches at the thickest point should be baked, fried, or poached for approximately 30 minutes. Cooking is done if the fish flakes easily when tested with a fork.

Broiling and Barbecuing

Grilling under a hot broiler and barbecuing over hot coals are fast, easy ways to prepare fish. Because these cooking methods involve high temperatures, slight basting usually is required to keep the fish moist. A marinade or some type of sauce coating may be used.

4

Arrange the fish in a single layer on a greased broiling rack or directly on a greased grill. Depending on the thickness of the fish, the rack or grill should be positioned for cooking 2 to 4 inches from the source of heat. Thinner pieces of fish are cooked closer to the heat; thicker fish or fish with a coating should cook further from the heat. The fish generally is turned only once during cooking, if indicated in the recipe. Fish suitable for broiling include: halibut, lobster, mackerel, red snapper, salmon, scrod, and whitefish.

Sautéing and Frying

Sautéing and frying also are quick-cooking methods for fish, but they may require a bit more preparation time than broiling or grilling. Before sautéing or frying, the fish is usually dipped into a liquid, such as milk or beaten eggs, then is either dusted with flour or rolled in cracker or bread crumbs.

A heavy skillet works well for pan-fried fish. If the fish is thick, cut a gash in the thickest part to shorten the cooking time. When deep-frying fish, oil should be heated to about 375°. Always drain sautéd or fried fish before serving. Fish suitable for frying include: catfish, flounder, ocean perch, smelt, sunfish, trout, and whiting.

Baking

Whole fish lend themselves particularly well to baking. Before baking a whole fish, remove the viscera, scales, fins, and, if desired, the head. Baked whole fish is ideal for stuffing; be creative and thrifty by using whatever ingredients are handy.

After cleaning the fish, lay it in a single layer in a large ovenproof baking dish; the fish should not be crowded. Coat the fish with oil or sauce or dot with butter, and be sure to baste the fish during cooking with accumulated pan juices. Fish generally is baked at 450°.

Fish suitable for baking include: bass, cod, red snapper, salmon, and whitefish.

Poaching and Steaming

Thick, firm fish or fillets are best for poaching. This method involves simmering the fish, below the boiling point, in a seasoned liquid called *court bouillon.* Poach fish in a special elongated pan, designed for this style of cooking, or improvise using cheesecloth and a large pot or roasting pan. Wrap the fish in the cheesecloth and suspend it from the handles of the pot during cooking. The cooking liquid should be simmering for at least 5 minutes before submersing the fish. Cover the pot while poaching. After poaching, drain off the liquid and remove the skin. Fish suitable for poaching include: cod, haddock, halibut, salmon, trout, and whitefish.

Steaming fish is a method similar to poaching, except the fish always stays above the level of the cooking liquid. Use a conventional steamer or improvise using a plate or rack in a covered pan. Invert a bowl in the bottom of a large pan. Add water, but do not cover the bowl. Arrange the fish in a single layer on a plate or on a greased rack that will fit inside the cooking pan; rest the plate or rack on the inverted bowl. Heat the water to boiling, then cover the pan to steam the fish. Fish suitable for steaming include: bluefish, cod, flounder, red snapper, and scrod.

APPETIZERS

SOUTH OF THE BORDER SHRIMP

Makes 10 servings

1 pound jumbo-sized shrimp (24 to 26 per pound)
1½ cups dry white wine
Boiling water
1 clove garlic, minced
1 lemon, sliced
4 sprigs parsley
Salt and pepper to taste
1 large apple
Mexican table sauce

In a large saucepan, cover shrimp with wine and boiling water. Add garlic, lemon, parsley, salt, and pepper; cook over medium heat for 3 to 5 minutes or until shrimp are pink. Drain shrimp; shell and devein. Skewer shrimp with wooden picks and spear into an apple to display. Serve with Mexican table sauce.

SEAFOOD QUICHE

Makes 6 servings

½ pound cooked lobster *or* crab, cut into ½-inch pieces
½ pound cooked shrimp, shelled, deveined, and cut into pieces
1 deep-dish frozen pie shell
½ cup sliced mushrooms
4 green onions, sliced
½ cup shredded sharp Cheddar cheese
4 eggs, lightly beaten
¼ cup sour cream
1 clove garlic, minced
¼ teaspoon tarragon

Preheat oven to 350°. Arrange lobster and shrimp in the bottom of pie shell. Sprinkle mushrooms and onions over seafood. Top with half of the cheese. In a small bowl, combine eggs, sour cream, garlic, and tarragon; mix well. Pour mixture over seafood. Sprinkle remaining cheese over all. Bake for 35 minutes or until a knife inserted in the center comes out clean.

SHRIMP PATÉ

Makes 6 servings

1 pound cooked shrimp, shelled and deveined
½ cup butter at room temperature
2 teaspoons horseradish
¼ teaspoon nutmeg
¼ teaspoon salt
2 tablespoons chopped fresh parsley
Assorted party breads *or* raw trimmed vegetables

Grind shrimp. In a mixing bowl, cream butter; blend in horseradish, nutmeg, and salt. Stir shrimp into butter mixture; pack into a 1½-cup mold. Chill until ready to serve. Unmold paté onto a serving dish; garnish with chopped parsley. Serve with bread or raw vegetables.

BROILED CRAB MEAT APPETIZERS

Makes 12 servings

2 cups cooked crab meat
  (remove gristle)
6 slices bacon, crisp-cooked and
  crumbled
1 teaspoon dry mustard
¼ teaspoon paprika
½ teaspoon celery salt
  Dash Worcestershire sauce
½ cup chili sauce
1 teaspoon red wine vinegar
1½ cups mayonnaise
1 package party rye bread

In a deep mixing bowl, combine all ingredients except the rye bread. Spread crab meat mixture on bread slices; arrange on a baking sheet. Broil appetizers until bubbly, about 30 seconds.

STEAMED NEW POTATOES WITH SOUR CREAM AND CAVIAR

Makes 12 servings

30 small, well-shaped, new
  potatoes, scrubbed
1½ cups sour cream
4 ounces yellow whitefish caviar

Arrange potatoes in a steamer over hot simmering water. Steam potatoes until tender, about 15 minutes. Scoop out a shallow depression in the top of each potato. Fill with sour cream and garnish with caviar. Serve hot or at room temperature. Filled potatoes may be reheated in the steamer for about 5 minutes before serving.

OYSTERS CASINO

Makes 4 servings

3 cups rock salt
16 oysters
1 red bell pepper, chopped
6 strips bacon, cut into 1½-inch
  pieces
1 lemon, cut into wedges
  Fresh seaweed, if available

Preheat oven to 400°. Spread rock salt in the bottom of a 9 x 13-inch baking dish; bake for 15 minutes. Open oysters; discard top shells; leave oysters and oyster liquor in the bottom shells. Arrange oysters securely in salt; sprinkle with chopped red pepper. Top each oyster with a piece of bacon. Bake for 15 minutes or until bacon is browned but not crisp. Garnish with lemon wedges. Serve oysters on a bed of seaweed.

HOT CLAM FONDUE

Makes 8 servings

4 cups shredded Cheddar cheese
¼ cup all-purpose flour
2 10¼-ounce cans frozen condensed New England clam chowder
1 8-ounce can minced clams, drained
1 small onion, chopped
French bread, cut into chunks

In a mixing bowl, stir together cheese and flour. In a large saucepan over medium heat, bring chowder to a simmer. Add cheese mixture; stir until cheese melts. Stir in clams and onion. Carefully pour mixture into a fondue pot. Serve with chunks of French bread for dipping.

OYSTERS ON THE HALF SHELL

Makes 6 servings

24 oysters in shells
Lemon wedges
Cocktail sauce
Horseradish
Vinegar
Oyster crackers

Open oysters; discard top shell. With a knife, cut oysters loose from bottom shells, being careful to retain liquor. Arrange oysters on a bed of crushed ice. Serve with lemon wedges, cocktail sauce, horseradish, vinegar, and oyster crackers.

BACON-WRAPPED SCALLOPS

Makes 4 to 6 servings

12 strips bacon, cut in half
24 raw scallops

In a skillet, sauté bacon until shrivelled but still limp. Wrap each scallop in a half slice of bacon and secure with a wooden pick. Broil scallops until bacon is crisp, about 5 minutes.

ITALIAN-STYLE SHRIMP

Makes 8 servings

2½ pounds medium shrimp, boiled, shelled, deveined, and chilled
2 teaspoons salt
½ teaspoon white pepper
1 cup olive oil
¾ cup minced parsley
1 tablespoon minced garlic
Parsley sprigs

With a sharp knife, slit shrimp ¾ through the back. In a deep mixing bowl, combine shrimp with salt and pepper; toss to mix. Stir in olive oil, parsley, and garlic; marinate shrimp and arrange on a bed of lettuce. Garnish with sprigs of parsley.

CLAM DIP WITH GARDEN VEGETABLES

Makes 6 to 8 servings

1 8-ounce package cream cheese
  at room temperature
1 cup sour cream
1 8-ounce can minced clams,
  drained (reserve liquid)
3 cloves garlic, minced
  Assorted raw vegetables

In a mixing bowl, beat cream cheese with sour cream until smooth. Fold in minced clams and garlic. Gradually stir in reserved clam liquid until dip is the desired consistency. Cover and chill until ready to serve. Serve with raw vegetables.

EASY FISH PATÉ

Makes 6 servings

½ pound smoked lake trout,
  skinned and boned
1 small tart apple, cored and
  grated
½ teaspoon horseradish
  Dash of lime juice
1 tablespoon finely chopped
  onion
1 clove garlic, minced
1 8-ounce package cream cheese
  at room temperature
¼ cup sliced mushrooms
  Crackers
  Raw vegetables

In a deep mixing bowl, mash trout with the back of a fork. Add apple; mix well. Blend in horseradish, lime juice, onion, garlic, and cream cheese. Mound mixture on a serving dish. Arrange mushrooms over top of paté. Serve with crackers and raw vegetables.

MAKE-AHEAD CRAB DELIGHT

Makes 6 servings

6 ounces Cheddar cheese spread
  at room temperature
1 6½-ounce can crab meat
  (remove gristle)
2 tablespoons butter at room
  temperature
1 tablespoon mayonnaise
3 green onions, chopped
⅛ teaspoon Worcestershire sauce
½ teaspoon lemon juice
6 English muffins, split into
  halves

In a mixing bowl, stir together all ingredients except the English muffins. Spread crab meat mixture on each muffin half; freeze in a single layer on a baking sheet. Stack frozen muffins, wrap in aluminum foil, and store in the freezer. Before serving, separate frozen muffins and thaw. Cut into quarters; bake at 350° for 10 minutes or until topping is bubbly.

Clam Dip with Garden Vegetables

SEVICHE

Makes 6 to 8 servings

1 pound bay scallops *or* sole
  fillets, cut into ¾-inch pieces
1 cup lemon juice
1 red onion, thinly sliced
½ teaspoon salt
½ teaspoon pepper
2 cloves garlic, minced
2 bay leaves
5 to 6 tablespoons olive oil
2 large tomatoes, peeled and
  chopped
2 tablespoons chopped fresh
  parsley

Place fish in a glass or ceramic bowl; pour in lemon juice. Add remaining ingredients; toss lightly to mix. Cover bowl loosely; marinate in refrigerator for 6 hours. Toss again; marinate for another 6 hours. Just before serving, adjust seasonings and toss. Serve in sherbet glasses.

SNAILS IN THE SHELL

Makes 6 servings

7 to 8 tablespoons butter at
  room temperature
3 cloves garlic, minced
1 tablespoon chopped shallots
  or green onion
1 tablespoon minced spinach
1 can large snails (18 to 20 snails
  per can), rinsed and drained
18 artificial snail shells (available
  at gourmet shops)
¼ cup seasoned bread crumbs

Preheat oven to 500°. In a mixing bowl, combine butter, garlic, shallots, and spinach. Roll snails in seasoned butter; stuff into shells. Fill shells with remaining butter; sprinkle with bread crumbs. Arrange snails, stuffing side up, in a snail baking dish or in a regular baking pan. Bake for 4 to 5 minutes. Serve immediately.

ROLLMOPS

Makes 4 servings

4 fillets matjes herring
2 teaspoons prepared mustard
1 kosher dill pickle, cut into 8
  thin strips
1 large red onion, thinly sliced
20 capers
1 cup dry white wine
½ cup white vinegar
1 tablespoon mixed whole
  pickling spices

Lay the herring fillets flat; spread a thin layer of mustard over each. Arrange 2 pickle strips, 3 onion rings, and 5 capers on each fillet. Roll up herring, jelly-roll style, and secure with wooden picks. In a flat glass or ceramic pan, combine wine, vinegar, pickling spices, and remaining onion. Arrange rollmops in the wine mixture; set aside to marinate for 3 days, turning occasionally. Drain and serve cold.

SOUPS, STEWS AND CHOWDERS

FISH STOCK

Makes 1½ quarts stock

2 pounds fish, including bones, heads, and skin
1 large onion, sliced
2 carrots, sliced
3 ribs celery, sliced
2 bay leaves
½ teaspoon thyme
4 peppercorns
1 cup dry white wine

Combine all ingredients in a stock pot. Add water to cover fish and vegetables. Bring mixture to a boil; reduce heat and simmer, uncovered, for 45 minutes. Strain through a double thickness of cheesecloth.

OYSTER BISQUE

Makes 6 servings

1 cup oysters
¼ cup cooked spinach
2 cups milk
1 cup half-and-half *or* heavy cream
½ teaspoon Worcestershire sauce
¼ teaspoon garlic powder
2 tablespoons butter
1 cup sour cream

In a blender or food processor, puree oysters and spinach; set aside. In a large saucepan over medium heat, combine milk and half-and-half; stir constantly until mixture simmers. Stir in oyster-spinach puree, Worcestershire sauce, and garlic powder. Add butter; simmer and stir until butter melts. Ladle bisque into 6 soup bowls; garnish each serving with a dollop of sour cream.

SOUTHERN GUMBO

Makes 6 servings

2 tablespoons bacon drippings
1 large onion, thinly sliced
2 cups chopped okra
3 large tomatoes, chopped
6 cups chicken stock
1 green pepper, thinly sliced
½ teaspoon red pepper flakes
2 bay leaves
Salt to taste
1 pound cooked shrimp, shelled and deveined
1 tablespoon filé powder
Hot cooked rice

In a large saucepan over medium-high heat, melt bacon drippings. Add onion and okra; sauté over medium heat until onion is tender. Stir in tomatoes and simmer for 4 to 5 minutes. Add chicken stock, green pepper, red pepper flakes, bay leaves, and salt. Bring mixture to a boil. Reduce heat and simmer, uncovered, for 10 minutes. Add shrimp, cover with tight-fitting lid, and continue cooking for 1 hour. Remove from heat. Discard bay leaves. Stir in filé powder. Serve over cooked rice.

13

SHRIMP BISQUE

Makes 4 to 6 servings

2 10½-ounce cans tomato soup
2 10½-ounce cans green pea
  soup
1 cup milk
1 cup cream
½ cup dry white wine
¾ pound cooked shrimp, shelled
  and deveined
  Croutons

In a large heavy saucepan over medium heat, combine soups, milk, and cream. Bring mixture to a boil, stirring occasionally. Add white wine and shrimp; bring to a simmer, stirring constantly. Garnish with croutons.

SAN FRANCISCO CIOPPINO

Makes 6 servings

1 onion, thinly sliced
1 small green pepper, cut into
  strips
3 cloves garlic, minced
4 tablespoons olive oil
4 large tomatoes, peeled and
  chopped
1 8-ounce can tomato sauce
2 cups fish stock (page 13)
2 bay leaves
½ teaspoon salt
½ teaspoon pepper
1 pound haddock fillet, cut into
  1-inch pieces
¾ pound shrimp, shelled and
  deveined
½ pound crab legs, cracked
  Sourdough bread

In a stock pot over medium heat, sauté onion, green pepper, and garlic in olive oil until tender. Stir in tomatoes, tomato sauce, and fish stock. Add bay leaves, salt, and pepper; simmer for 10 minutes. Add haddock, shrimp, and crab; simmer, stirring occasionally, for 10 minutes or until haddock flakes easily. Serve with sourdough bread.

ORIENTAL ABALONE SOUP

Makes 4 servings

4 cups chicken stock
½ teaspoon ground ginger
3 green onions, chopped
1 small carrot, grated
  Salt and pepper to taste
½ cup sliced canned abalone,
  drained and shredded
¼ cup minced fresh parsley

Bring chicken stock to a boil in a large saucepan. Stir in remaining ingredients, except abalone and parsley. Reduce heat; simmer for 15 minutes. Stir in abalone. Simmer until heated through; ladle into soup bowls. Sprinkle with parsley.

San Francisco Cioppino

NEW ENGLAND FISH CHOWDER

Makes 8 servings

3 slices bacon
1 large onion, chopped
3 ribs celery, sliced
1 carrot, thinly sliced
4 potatoes, peeled and cut into
½-inch cubes
1½ pounds assorted firm-fleshed
fish fillets (such as haddock *or*
halibut), boned and cut into
1-inch pieces
2 cups hot water
1 teaspoon salt
½ teaspoon white pepper
3 cups milk
2 cups half-and-half
3 tablespoons butter
Saltines

In a large skillet over medium heat, cook bacon. Remove bacon, crumble, and set aside. To bacon drippings, add onion, celery, and carrot; sauté until tender. Add potatoes, fish, and hot water. Simmer, uncovered, for 20 minutes, stirring occasionally. Season with salt and pepper. Add milk, half-and-half, and butter; simmer, stirring constantly, until chowder is hot and butter melts. Sprinkle with crumbled bacon and serve with saltines.

BOUILLABAISSE

Makes 8 servings

3 tablespoons butter
3 tablespoons olive oil
3 cloves garlic, minced
1 large onion, thinly sliced
2 ribs celery, sliced
4 large tomatoes, peeled and
chopped
4 cups tomato juice
2 cups clam juice
½ pound mushrooms, sliced
5 bay leaves
1 teaspoon salt
½ teaspoon ground black pepper
¼ teaspoon saffron
3 pounds firm-fleshed fish fillets
(such as red snapper *or* sea
bass), cut into 2-inch pieces
1 pound shrimp
1 pound scallops
12 mussels in shells, debearded
1 pound king crab legs, split and
cut into 3-inch pieces
1 small loaf French bread, sliced

In a stockpot over medium heat, melt butter with olive oil. Add garlic, onion, and celery; sauté until vegetables are tender. Stir in tomatoes, tomato juice, clam juice, mushrooms, bay leaves, salt, pepper, and saffron; simmer 5 minutes. Add fish pieces; simmer 15 minutes. Add shrimp, scallops, mussels, and crab. Simmer, uncovered, for 10 minutes or until fish flakes easily when tested with a fork. Adjust seasonings; discard bay leaves. Place a slice of bread in each soup bowl. Ladle bouillabaisse into bowls.

OYSTER STEW

Makes 6 servings

5 tablespoons butter *or* margarine
1 pint oysters, drained
1 pint heavy cream
1 pint half-and-half
½ teaspoon salt
½ teaspoon white pepper
4 tablespoons dry sherry
   Saltines

In a large heavy saucepan, melt butter. Add oysters and simmer until edges curl. In a separate medium saucepan, heat heavy cream and half-and-half, stirring constantly, only until warm. Blend warm cream into oyster-butter mixture. Season with salt and pepper. Stir in sherry. Serve with saltines.

SOUTHERN SNAPPER SOUP

Makes 8 servings

4 tablespoons butter
1 onion, thinly sliced
1 green pepper, sliced
4 ribs celery, sliced
1½ cups bite-sized pieces red
   snapper fillets
2 cups fish stock (page 13)
2 cups tomato sauce
½ cup dry sherry
½ teaspoon thyme
½ teaspoon oregano
   Salt and pepper to taste
¼ cup chopped fresh parsley

In a large heavy saucepan over medium heat, melt butter. Add onion, green pepper, and celery; sauté until tender. Add red snapper; simmer for 3 minutes. Blend in remaining ingredients, except parsley; simmer for 5 minutes. Serve hot, sprinkled with parsley.

MANHATTAN CLAM CHOWDER

Makes 6 servings

4 slices bacon
1 large onion, thinly sliced
3 ribs celery, sliced
3 potatoes, peeled and cubed
½ teaspoon thyme
½ teaspoon salt
½ teaspoon pepper
2 8-ounce cans tomatoes,
   with juice
2 cups clam juice
2 7-ounce cans minced clams,
   with juice
   Oyster crackers

In a large saucepan over medium-high heat, cook bacon until crisp. Remove bacon; drain and crumble for garnish. Pour off all but 4 tablespoons of drippings. Add onion, celery, and potatoes; sauté until celery and onion are tender, stirring often. Season with thyme, salt, and pepper. Blend in tomatoes (with juice) and clam juice. Break up tomatoes. Simmer uncovered for 30 minutes or until potatoes are tender. Stir in clams (with liquid). Continue simmering for 5 minutes. Adjust seasonings. Ladle into serving bowls and sprinkle with crumbled bacon. Serve with oyster crackers.

SALADS

HADDOCK SALAD IN TOMATO CUPS

Makes 6 servings

3 cups flaked cooked haddock
4 green onions, chopped
3 hard-cooked eggs, chopped
3 tablespoons sweet pickle relish
½ cup diced celery
½ cup blanched bean sprouts
½ cup mayonnaise
6 whole tomatoes
   Black olives
   Parsley sprigs

In a deep bowl, combine all ingredients except tomatoes, olives, and parsley; toss lightly to mix. Cut a slice off the top of each tomato; carefully scoop out centers. (Zigzag edges, if desired.) Mound haddock mixture in tomato cups. Garnish with black olives and parsley.

CRAB AND SHRIMP SALAD

Makes 6 servings

1½ pounds shrimp, cooked, deveined, and chopped
1 6½-ounce can crab meat (remove gristle)
4 ribs celery, chopped
5 hard-cooked eggs
1 3-ounce package cream cheese at room temperature
   Mayonnaise
   Catsup
   Salt and white pepper to taste
½ teaspoon Tabasco
2 cloves garlic, minced
   Lettuce leaves

Place shrimp, crab meat, and celery in a large serving bowl; stir to mix. In a separate small bowl, mash egg whites with a fork; add to seafood mixture. In same small bowl, mash egg yolks and blend with cream cheese. Add mayonnaise and catsup to taste. Season with salt, pepper, Tabasco, and garlic. Stir into seafood mixture. Serve over lettuce.

HERRING SALAD

Makes 8 servings

1 16-ounce jar pickled herring fillets, drained (reserve liquid)
2 slices white bread, crusts removed
2 large cooking apples, peeled and grated
4 hard-cooked eggs, chopped
   Sliced tomatoes
   Pumpernickel

Mince herring. In a large mixing bowl, soak bread in reserved liquid until all liquid is absorbed, about 10 minutes. Stir in herring, apples, and eggs. Cover mixture and chill until ready to serve. Garnish with sliced tomatoes and serve with pumpernickel.

18

CRAB MOUSSE

Makes 8 servings

2 envelopes unflavored gelatin
1 cup cold water
1 10½-ounce can tomato soup
4 ounces cream cheese at room temperature
1 tablespoon lemon juice
1 small onion, chopped
1 cup mayonnaise
1 cup chopped celery
¼ cup diced black olives
1 small green pepper, finely chopped
1 cup flaked crab meat or lobster
Fresh vegetables
Mayonnaise

Soften gelatin in ½ cup of the cold water. In a medium saucepan over medium heat, cook tomato soup to a simmer. Stir in softened gelatin and cream cheese; simmer and stir until mixture is smooth. Stir in remaining water, lemon juice, and onion. Chill mixture until partially set. Fold in mayonnaise, celery, olives, green pepper, and crab meat. Spoon mixture into a lightly greased loaf pan or fish mold. Chill until firm. Unmold. Garnish with fresh vegetables and serve with extra mayonnaise.

SALAD-STUFFED CROISSANTS

Makes 6 servings

1 6½-ounce can tuna, drained and flaked
½ cup chopped celery
½ cup mayonnaise
3 tablespoons chopped sweet pickles
1 small green pepper, chopped
6 croissants

Preheat oven to 350°. In a deep mixing bowl, combine all ingredients except croissants. Toss to mix. Split croissants; remove inside dough, leaving a thin shell. Mound tuna filling loosely in rolls. Place filled croissants on a cookie sheet. Bake for 5 to 10 minutes or until heated through.

TROPICAL TUNA SALAD

Makes 4 servings

1 6½-ounce can tuna, drained and flaked
1 13-ounce can pineapple chunks, drained
½ cup slivered almonds
½ cup raisins
¼ cup grated coconut
1 small red onion, thinly sliced
½ cup mayonnaise
4 tablespoons catsup
¼ teaspoon salt
1 small head romaine lettuce

In a large mixing bowl, combine tuna with remaining ingredients, except lettuce. Arrange lettuce leaves on individual plates. Top with tuna salad. Chill until ready to serve.

SEAFOOD TOMATO ASPIC

Makes 8 servings

3 3-ounce packages cream cheese
  at room temperature
1 10½-ounce can tomato soup
1 cup mayonnaise
¾ cup chopped cooked shrimp
¾ cup chopped cooked scallops
1 green pepper, chopped
1 small red onion, chopped
3 ribs celery, sliced
½ teaspoon garlic powder
1 envelope unflavored gelatin
¼ cup cold water
  Lettuce
  Tomatoes

In a deep bowl, blend cream cheese with tomato soup and mayonnaise until smooth. Stir in shrimp, scallops, vegetables, and garlic powder; set aside. In a small saucepan, soften gelatin in cold water. Over medium heat, stir gelatin until dissolved, then add to seafood mixture. Pour mixture into lightly oiled mold. Cover and chill until firm. Unmold onto a bed of lettuce and tomatoes.

TUNA MOLD

Makes 8 servings

1 envelope unflavored gelatin
½ cup cold water
1 10½-ounce can tomato soup
1 8-ounce package cream cheese
2 6½-ounce cans tuna, drained
1 cup mayonnaise
¾ cup chopped celery
¾ cup chopped green onions
½ teaspoon Worcestershire sauce
2 cloves garlic, minced
  Lettuce leaves, sliced tomatoes,
  and black olives for garnish

Soften gelatin in cold water; set aside. In a medium saucepan over medium heat, combine tomato soup and cream cheese; blend well. Add softened gelatin; stir until dissolved; set aside to cool. Add remaining ingredients to tomato soup mixture. Pour into a lightly oiled 1½-quart mold (or individual molds, if desired). Cover and chill until firm. Unmold onto a bed of lettuce leaves on a chilled serving platter. Garnish with tomatoes and black olives.

LOBSTER SALAD FOR SANDWICHES

Makes 6 servings

2 6½-ounce cans lobster
  (remove gristle), flaked
3 hard-cooked eggs, chopped
½ cup sliced black olives
1 small onion, chopped
2 tablespoons chopped sweet
  pickle
¾ cup mayonnaise
½ teaspoon salt
2 teaspoons minced fresh parsley
6 sandwich rolls

In a large mixing bowl, toss together all ingredients except rolls. Chill mixture in refrigerator until ready to serve. Serve in sandwich rolls.

SALMON MOUSSE

Makes 8 to 10 servings

1 envelope unflavored gelatin
½ cup hot water
1 16-ounce can red sockeye salmon (bones and skin removed), flaked
½ cup mayonnaise
2 tablespoons lime juice
3 green onions, chopped
1 cup heavy cream
  Lettuce leaves
1 cucumber, thinly sliced
1 rib celery, sliced
  Stuffed green olives, pimiento, apples, and oranges
  Sour Cream Sauce

Soften gelatin in water. In a mixing bowl, combine softened gelatin, salmon, mayonnaise, lime juice, and onions; mix well. Gradually stir in cream. Mound mixture in a lightly greased 5-cup fish mold. Cover with aluminum foil and chill overnight. Just before serving, unmold onto a serving platter. Surround mousse with lettuce leaves. Arrange cucumber and celery slices in a scale-like pattern over mousse. Use olive slices for eyes, pimiento strips for mouth and tail. Garnish with sliced apples and oranges. Serve with Sour Cream Sauce.

SOUR CREAM SAUCE

Makes 2 cups sauce

1 small onion, finely chopped
1 cup mayonnaise
1 cup sour cream
1 tablespoon prepared mustard
1 tablespoon lime juice *or* lemon juice
1 sprig fresh dill *or* 1 teaspoon dill seed

Combine all ingredients; stir until well mixed. Place in a covered dish; refrigerate until needed.

EASY SHRIMP SALAD

Makes 6 servings

2 cups shell macaroni, uncooked
1½ cups frozen shrimp, thawed
1 cup diced celery
1 cup sour cream
2 tablespoons prepared horseradish
2 tablespoons minced onion
½ teaspoon dry mustard
½ teaspoon salt
  Dash marjoram
6 artichokes, steamed and cored (optional)

Cook shell macaroni according to package directions; drain. Rinse with cold water to cool quickly; drain well. In a large bowl, toss together macaroni, shrimp, and celery. In a separate small bowl, combine sour cream, horseradish, onion, and the seasonings; whisk until well blended and of a creamy consistency. Pour dressing over macaroni mixture; toss lightly until blended. Chill. Serve in hollowed artichokes, if desired.

Easy Shrimp Salad

SEAFOOD PASTA SALAD

Makes 6 servings

3 tablespoons butter
½ cup dry white wine
¾ pound scallops, halved if larger than bite-size
1 cup half-and-half
½ cup mayonnaise
2 teaspoons red wine vinegar
2 tablespoons chopped fresh basil
Salt and pepper to taste
¾ pound fettucini, cooked according to package directions, drained
½ pound shrimp, cooked, shelled, and deveined

In a saucepan over medium heat, melt butter. Stir in wine and scallops; reduce heat and simmer until scallops are tender, about 3 minutes. Remove scallops from wine. Cook wine over high heat for 1 minute; remove from heat; set aside. In a deep bowl, combine half-and-half, mayonnaise, wine vinegar, basil, salt, and pepper. Stir in wine. In a serving bowl, toss pasta, scallops, and shrimp with sauce. Serve cold or at room temperature.

SALAD NICOISE

Makes 6 servings

1 medium head iceberg lettuce, shredded
3 large tomatoes, peeled and cut into wedges
1 cucumber, peeled and sliced
1 red onion, thinly sliced
3 large potatoes, cooked, peeled and sliced
½ pound string beans, cooked and chilled
1 cup whole pitted ripe olives
2 2-ounce cans anchovies, drained and flaked
2 6½-ounce cans tuna, drained and broken into chunks
1 medium lemon, thinly sliced
Garlic Vinaigrette

In a deep mixing bowl, toss lettuce, tomatoes, cucumber, and onion; arrange on 6 individual chilled salad plates. Arrange potato slices, string beans, and olives attractively on top of lettuce mixture. Cross anchovies over each salad serving. Arrange tuna and lemon slices over salad. Drizzle with Garlic Vinaigrette.

GARLIC VINAIGRETTE

3 cloves garlic, minced
3 tablespoons wine vinegar
½ teaspoon dry mustard
½ teaspoon salt
¼ teaspoon ground pepper
3 tablespoons vegetable oil
3 tablespoons olive oil

In a small mixing bowl, beat together all ingredients until well mixed. Drizzle over salad.

— BROILED AND — GRILLED

LOBSTER THERMIDOR

Makes 2 servings

1 whole lobster (about 1 pound)
  or 2 lobster tails
1 tablespoon butter
4 mushrooms, sliced
2 green onions, minced
1 cup heavy cream
  Salt, pepper, dry mustard, and
  cayenne pepper to taste
½ cup grated Swiss cheese
3 tablespoons Parmesan cheese

Drop lobster into a pot of boiling water; boil 8 to 10 minutes. Remove lobster; set aside to cool. Place lobster on its back on a cutting board; cut in half lengthwise, through the shell. Pull out and discard the sac behind the eyes. Discard the green liver. Break off the 2 large claws; crack with a knife and remove meat. Remove meat from tail. Set shell aside. Cut meat into 1-inch cubes. In a skillet over low heat, melt butter. Add mushrooms and green onions; cook for 5 minutes. Add lobster meat; cook until warmed, about 5 minutes.

In a small skillet, bring cream to a boil. Boil rapidly until cream is reduced by half and coats a spoon. Remove from heat. Season to taste with salt, pepper, mustard, and cayenne. Stir in Swiss cheese, lobster, and vegetables. Spoon mixture into lobster shells; sprinkle with Parmesan cheese. Broil, 6 inches from heat, until lightly browned.

GRILLED SPICY SWORDFISH

Makes 6 servings

¾ cup plain yogurt
3 tablespoons tomato paste
1 tablespoon peanut oil
4 tablespoons lemon juice
4 tablespoons minced onion
2 cloves garlic, minced
½ teaspoon ground ginger
½ teaspoon coriander
½ teaspoon cumin
½ teaspoon turmeric
¼ teaspoon ground cloves
2¼ pounds swordfish, cut into
  serving-sized pieces

In a mixing bowl, stir together all ingredients except swordfish. Place swordfish in a shallow baking dish; cover with seasoning mixture and marinate for 2 hours, turning occasionally. Place marinated swordfish in an oiled hinged wire basket. Grill about 4 inches from hot coals for 15 minutes, turning occasionally and basting with marinade.

GRILLED WALLEYE PIKE

Makes 6 servings

1 whole walleye pike (about 4½ pounds), cleaned, scaled, and deboned; leave skin intact
Juice of 3 oranges
2 cloves garlic, minced
¾ teaspoon white pepper
¾ teaspoon oregano
½ cup olive oil

Place fish in a shallow bowl. Stir together orange juice, garlic, pepper, and oregano; spread over fish. Marinate fish in juice mixture for 30 minutes. Open fish along cut made for filleting; keep halves attached. Place opened fish on an oiled grill or in an oiled hinged wire basket. Grill fish about 6 inches from medium-hot coals for about 8 minutes on each side, brushing alternately with juice mixture and olive oil. Grill until fish flakes easily when tested with a fork.

GRILLED SCROD

Makes 6 servings

¼ cup peanut oil
¼ cup lime juice
½ teaspoon salt
Dash Worcestershire sauce
1 tablespoon onion flakes
2¼ pounds scrod fillets, cut into serving-sized pieces
Paprika
Parsley, black olives, and lemon wedges for garnish

In a small bowl, stir together all ingredients, except fillets and garnishes. Arrange fillets in a shallow dish. Pour oil mixture over fillets and marinate for 1½ hours, turning twice. Transfer fillets to an oiled wire basket; brush with marinade. Grill fillets 4 to 5 inches from medium-hot coals for about 6 minutes or until fish flakes easily when tested with a fork. Baste fish with marinade during cooking. Before serving, dust with paprika; garnish with parsley, black olives, and lemon wedges.

GRILLED LOBSTER TAILS

Makes 4 servings

4 large rock lobster tails
¼ pound butter, melted

Loosen meat from lobster tails leaving shells intact. Force a small skewer lengthwise through each lobster tail, causing it to straighten. Brush lobsters with melted butter and place, shell side down, on a grill 4 to 5 inches from hot coals. Grill for 8 to 10 minutes or until shells begin to char. Turn once and grill for 3 more minutes. Serve with extra melted butter.

Grilled Scrod

SHRIMP ON THE GRILL

Makes 6 servings

1 cup Barbecue Sauce for Shrimp
½ teaspoon red pepper flakes
2½ pounds medium *or* large
    shrimp, shelled and deveined
    (leave tail attached)

Prepare Barbecue Sauce for Shrimp. In a shallow bowl, stir together barbecue sauce and red pepper flakes. Thread shrimp on 6 skewers and place on a lightly oiled grill about 5 inches from hot coals. Brush shrimp with barbecue sauce, turn, and brush again with sauce. Grill about 3 to 4 minutes on each side.

BARBECUE SAUCE FOR SHRIMP

Makes 1¾ cups sauce

⅓ cup wine vinegar
1 cup tomato juice
4 tablespoons light brown sugar
1 teaspoon prepared mustard
2 cloves garlic, minced
  Salt and pepper to taste
1 small onion, thinly sliced
¼ cup catsup
1 teaspoon Worcestershire sauce

In a small saucepan, combine all ingredients, except catsup and Worcestershire sauce. Simmer, uncovered, for 10 minutes. Stir in catsup and Worcestershire sauce; bring mixture to a boil. Place in a covered container and refrigerate until ready to use.

BARBECUED TROUT

Makes 6 servings

6 small whole trout, cleaned
½ pound bacon

Wash trout and pat dry with paper towels. Wrap trout in bacon slices; place in an oiled wire basket. Cook over hot coals about 4 inches from heat, turning as necessary. Fish is ready when bacon is crisp and fish flakes easily when tested with a fork.

ON THE GRILL FISH PACKETS

Makes 6 servings

6 serving-sized pieces
  swordfish
  Salt and pepper to taste
1 onion, sliced
1 medium zucchini, thinly sliced

Cut 6 pieces of aluminum foil, each twice the size of one piece of fish. Place fish in center of aluminum foil; sprinkle with salt and pepper. Scatter onion and zucchini over fish. Fold foil securely, envelope style, around fish. Grill about 4 inches from coals for 6 to 9 minutes, depending on thickness of fish. Serve fish wrapped in packets.

BROILED BASS WITH MUSHROOMS AND ONIONS

Makes 6 servings

2¼ pounds striped bass fillets
¼ cup peanut oil
¼ cup toasted sesame seeds
3 tablespoons lime juice
¼ cup sake *or* dry white wine
3 tablespoons light soy sauce
½ teaspoon garlic powder
3 tablespoons peanut oil
2 cups sliced mushrooms
6 green onions, sliced into
　1½-inch pieces

Arrange fish fillets in a shallow glass dish. Combine all remaining ingredients, except 3 tablespoons oil, mushrooms, and onions, making a marinade. Drizzle marinade over the fish fillets and set aside at room temperature for 1½ hours, turning fish once. Place fillets, skin side down, on a greased broiling pan. Broil about 4 inches from heat for 7 to 8 minutes or until fish flakes easily when tested with a fork. Transfer fish to a warm serving platter. In a heavy skillet over medium heat, sauté mushrooms and onions in peanut oil until tender. Arrange vegetables around and over fish.

BROILED LOBSTER TAILS

Makes 6 servings

6 lobster tails, thawed
¼ pound butter, melted
½ teaspoon dried tarragon
1 lemon, cut into wedges

Place lobster tails on a broiler rack, shell side up, 4 to 5 inches from heat. Broil for 5 minutes. Turn, brush with butter, and broil for 7 minutes more. Transfer to warmed dinner plates. Stir tarragon into remaining butter. Serve lobster with seasoned butter and lemon wedges.

FRENCH-STYLE FISH FILLETS

Makes 5 to 6 servings

2 pounds fish fillets
¾ cup dry white wine
2 cloves garlic, minced
4 tablespoons chopped fresh
　parsley
½ teaspoon basil
½ teaspoon thyme
¼ teaspoon paprika
1 tablespoon lemon juice
　Salt and pepper to taste
3 tablespoons butter, in chunks

Line an 11 x 7-inch baking pan with aluminum foil. Arrange fish fillets in a single layer in the pan. Combine remaining ingredients, except butter. Sprinkle fish with herb mixture and set aside for 30 minutes. Dot fish with butter and place under broiler. Broil, without turning, about 4 inches from heat for about 8 minutes or until fish flakes easily when tested with a fork.

SCALLOP KABOBS

Makes 8 servings

½ cup light soy sauce
½ cup light brown sugar
¼ cup wine vinegar
¼ cup orange juice
½ teaspoon salt
2 cloves garlic, minced
2 pounds large scallops
2 red bell peppers, cut into
  24 squares
2 medium onions, cut into
  24 wedges
2 large tomatoes, each cut
  into eighths
  Rice *or* noodles

In a large saucepan over medium heat, combine all ingredients, except scallops, vegetables, and rice. Bring to a boil, stirring constantly. Remove from heat and cool to room temperature. Place scallops in a large flat casserole; cover with sauce and marinate in refrigerator for 3 hours. Thread scallops, peppers, onions, and tomatoes on 8 skewers. Broil 4 inches from heat for about 5 minutes on each side or until scallops are cooked. Serve over rice or noodles.

BROILED RED SNAPPER

Makes 4 servings

2 pounds red snapper fillets
  Salt, pepper, and garlic powder
  to taste
  Juice of one lemon
3 tablespoons butter, melted
2 teaspoons grated lemon peel
4 tablespoons Grand Marnier

Arrange red snapper fillets in an ovenproof baking dish; season with salt, pepper, and garlic powder. Drizzle lemon juice and melted butter over fillets and sprinkle with lemon peel. Broil fillets about 4 inches from heat for 5 to 8 minutes, depending on size of fish; baste with accumulated juices. If fillets are thick, turn once during cooking time. Drizzle with Grand Marnier and serve.

SHRIMP AND SCALLOPS EN BROCHETTE

Makes 6 servings

1 pound sea scallops
1 pound shrimp, shelled and
  deveined (leave tail attached)
½ pound mushrooms
1 green pepper, cubed
1 medium onion, cut into wedges
1 cup pineapple chunks, drained
6 strips bacon, cut into 2-inch
  pieces
  Bottled French *or* Italian salad
  dressing

On 6 skewers, thread whole scallops, shrimp, mushrooms, green pepper, onion, pineapple, and bacon. Grill over charcoal or cook under the broiler 4 inches from heat for about 10 minutes. Turn often and baste with salad dressing.

Shrimp and Scallops en Brochette

BROILED SALMON WITH DILL SAUCE

Makes 3 servings

6 4-ounce salmon fillets
Dry white wine
4 tablespoons butter, melted
Dill Sauce

Arrange salmon fillets skin side down in a broiler-proof shallow baking dish. Add wine to a depth of half the thickness of the fillets. Brush the tops of fillets with butter. Broil about 4 inches from heat just until fillets flake easily when tested with a fork. Transfer to a heated platter. Drizzle Dill Sauce over salmon.

DILL SAUCE

1 cup dry white wine
¼ cup white vinegar
¼ small onion, minced
¾ cup heavy cream
¾ pound unsalted butter at room temperature
Salt and white pepper to taste
1 tablespoon minced fresh dill

In a heavy saucepan over medium heat, bring wine, vinegar, and onion to a boil. Reduce heat and simmer until the liquid is reduced to about 1 tablespoon. Stir in cream; simmer, stirring constantly, until sauce is reduced by half. Remove from heat. Add bits of softened butter; stir until sauce is smooth. Season to taste with salt and white pepper. Stir in dill just before serving.

BROILED FISH STEAKS WITH HORSERADISH SAUCE

Makes 6 servings

2 pounds whitefish steaks
3 tablespoons chopped fresh parsley
½ cup teriyaki sauce
Horseradish Sauce

Arrange a single layer of fish steaks in a shallow pan; sprinkle with parsley. Pour teriyaki sauce over fish and set aside to marinate for 5 minutes, turning once. Broil the fish steaks 6 inches from heat for 4 minutes on each side or until fish flakes easily when tested with a fork. Brush fish steaks with marinade after turning. Serve with Horseradish Sauce.

HORSERADISH SAUCE

Makes 1½ cups sauce

½ cup prepared horseradish
1 tablespoon all-purpose flour
½ teaspoon salt
1 cup half-and-half or cream

In a small saucepan over medium heat, combine horseradish, flour, and salt. Stir in half-and-half. Cook and stir until mixture thickens slightly.

SAUTÉD AND FRIED

SAUTÉD SOLE WITH ASPARAGUS

Makes 6 servings

18 medium-sized asparagus spears
6 6-ounce fillets of sole
  Salt and pepper to taste
  All-purpose flour
3 eggs, lightly beaten
½ cup butter
1 cup Hollandaise Sauce
  (page 53)

Steam the asparagus spears just until tender; set aside. Season fish with salt and pepper. Roll fillets in flour to coat lightly; dip in beaten eggs. In a large skillet, melt ¼ cup of the butter over medium heat. Bring heat to high; add fillets and sauté until golden on each side. Transfer to heated dinner plates; keep warm. Melt remaining butter; add asparagus and sauté just until warmed. Arrange 3 spears across each fillet. Top with Hollandaise Sauce.

SAUTÉD MAHI MAHI

Makes 6 servings

½ cup peanut oil
2 pounds mahi mahi, cod, *or*
  other thick fish, cut into
  serving-sized pieces
  All-purpose flour
6 tablespoons butter
4 ounces sliced almonds
  Canned pineapple slices

In a large skillet, heat peanut oil to 350°. Dust mahi mahi with flour; sauté in oil on both sides until cooked and golden brown, about 3 minutes. Drain; transfer to a warmed platter and set aside. In a medium saucepan, melt butter; cook until light brown. Add almonds; sauté until browned and crisp. Sprinkle almonds over fish. Garnish with pineapple slices.

DELICATE TURBOT SAUTÉ

Makes 2 servings

½ cup orange juice
¼ cup dry white wine
2 tablespoons honey
½ cup butter
1 clove garlic, minced
½ teaspoon ground ginger
1 pound turbot fillets, cut into
  bite-sized pieces
½ cup slivered almonds
  Hot cooked rice
  Orange and lime slices

In a small bowl, combine orange juice, wine, and honey; stir until well blended; set aside. In a large skillet, melt butter. Add garlic and ginger; sauté about 15 seconds. Add turbot and almonds; sauté until almonds are golden. Pour juice mixture into skillet; simmer 3 minutes or until heated through. Serve over rice. Garnish with orange and lime slices.

33

SAUTÉD ORANGE ROUGHY WITH RIPE OLIVES

Makes 4 servings

4 tablespoons butter
1 tablespoon peanut oil
2 pounds orange roughy fillets
  Salt and pepper to taste
½ teaspoon tarragon
3 tablespoons all-purpose flour
1½ cups heavy cream
¼ cup chopped black olives

In a large skillet over medium heat, melt 2 tablespoons of the butter with the peanut oil. Season fillets with salt, pepper, and tarragon. Sauté on both sides until cooked, turning once. Transfer fish to a heated platter and keep warm. Melt remaining butter and blend in flour. Add cream; heat, stirring constantly, until sauce thickens. Stir in black olives. Drizzle sauce over fish.

SHRIMP SAUTÉ

Makes 5 to 6 servings

3 tablespoons butter
2 pounds shrimp, shelled and deveined
1 cup sliced mushrooms
3 tablespoons chopped fresh parsley
1 cup dry white wine
1 cup heavy cream
  Garlic toast

In a heavy skillet over medium heat, melt butter until it sizzles. Add shrimp; sauté until opaque. Stir in mushrooms; sauté for 1 minute. Remove shrimp and mushrooms from skillet; transfer to a platter, sprinkle with parsley, and keep warm. Add wine; simmer, stirring constantly, until volume is reduced by half. Stir in heavy cream; cook and stir for 3 minutes. Drizzle sauce over shrimp. Serve with garlic toast.

FISHERMAN'S SPECIAL

Makes 4 servings

4 rainbow trout (about 8 ounces each), filleted
  Salt and pepper to taste
6 tablespoons butter
1 large onion, sliced
3 large tomatoes, cut into wedges

Season cavity of trout with salt and pepper. In a large skillet over medium heat, melt 3 tablespoons of the butter until it sizzles. Add trout; fry for 2 to 3 minutes. Add remaining butter, turn trout, and continue to cook for 2 minutes or until fish flakes easily when tested with a fork. Transfer fish to a warmed serving platter. Reheat butter in skillet, adding more if necessary. Add onion; sauté until tender. Add tomatoes and heat through. Arrange cooked vegetables around fish.

Shrimp Sauté

BUTTERFISH MEUNIERE

Makes 5 to 6 servings

4 tablespoons butter
1 teaspoon peanut oil
1¾ pounds butterfish fillets
½ cup milk
½ cup all-purpose flour
  Salt and pepper to taste
4 tablespoons lemon juice
4 tablespoons chopped fresh
  parsley
4 tablespoons thyme
4 tablespoons rosemary

In a large heavy skillet over medium heat, melt 3 tablespoons of the butter with the peanut oil. Dip fish fillets in milk, roll lightly in flour, and season with salt and pepper. Sauté fish on both sides until cooked, turning once. Transfer to a heated platter and keep warm. Melt remaining butter; stir in lemon juice and herbs. Drizzle sauce over fish.

FISH FRY

Makes 8 to 10 servings

1 pound large shrimp, shelled and
  deveined (leave tail attached)
2 pounds flounder fillets, cut
  into strips
2 pounds red snapper fillets,
  cut into strips
½ cup dry white wine
2 cups all-purpose flour
2 eggs, lightly beaten
1 cup milk
  Salt, pepper, and garlic powder
  to taste
3 cups peanut oil for deep frying
1 lime, sliced

Wash shrimp and fish fillets; pat dry with paper towels. Sprinkle wine over fish; dust with ½ cup of the flour. In a shallow bowl, combine remaining flour, eggs, milk, salt, pepper, and garlic powder; stir until well blended. Set batter aside at room temperature for 30 minutes. In a medium skillet, heat oil to 375°. Dip shrimp and fish into batter, a few pieces at a time. Carefully slide into oil. Fry until golden brown on both sides, turning once. Drain on paper towels; transfer to a serving platter. Keep warm while frying remaining fish. Garnish with lime slices.

FRIED FISH IN CORNMEAL

Makes 6 servings

2 pounds flounder fillets
1 teaspoon salt
½ teaspoon pepper
½ teaspoon celery salt
¼ cup milk
½ cup all-purpose flour
½ cup yellow cornmeal
  Peanut oil
  Parsley sprigs

Wash fish and pat dry with paper towels. In a shallow bowl, combine salt, pepper, celery salt, milk, flour, and cornmeal; mix well. In a heavy skillet, heat 4 tablespoons peanut oil. Dip fish in batter; fry, turning once, until golden brown and tender. Garnish with parsley sprigs.

FISH AND CHIPS

Makes 6 servings

2 cups all-purpose flour
2 eggs, separated
¼ cup light beer
½ teaspoon salt
¼ cup milk
¼ cup water
1½ pounds medium-large potatoes, peeled and cut into ¼-inch slices
2 cups peanut oil
2 pounds flounder, sole, *or* haddock fillets, cut into serving-sized pieces
Wine vinegar
Tartar sauce

In a mixing bowl, beat together flour, egg yolks, beer, and salt. Beat in milk and water; stir until smooth. Set aside for 20 minutes. Rinse potatoes in cold water and pat dry. In a deep saucepan, heat oil to 375°. Fry potatoes, a few at a time, until tender, but not browned (about 4 minutes). Drain potatoes on paper toweling, cover with waxed paper, and set aside. Keep oil hot. Beat egg whites until stiff; fold into batter. Dip fish into batter; fry in hot oil, a few pieces at a time, until golden brown, turning as necessary. Drain on paper towels, transfer to a platter, and keep warm in a 300° oven. Increase oil heat to 390°. Fry potatoes, a few at a time, until crisp and browned. Drain on paper towels and sprinkle lightly with salt. Serve fish and chips warm with wine vinegar and tartar sauce.

STIR-FRIED SHRIMP WITH LOBSTER SAUCE

Makes 4 to 5 servings

1½ pounds shrimp, shelled and deveined
1 tablespoon white wine
Salt and pepper to taste
6 tablespoons peanut oil
2 cloves garlic, minced
½ teaspoon ground ginger
3 green onions, chopped
1 tablespoon fermented black beans (available in Oriental food stores), washed, rinsed, and mashed
½ pound ground pork
1 green pepper, sliced
2 teaspoons cornstarch
5 teaspoons soy sauce
½ cup chicken stock
1 teaspoon sesame oil
2 eggs, beaten
Hot cooked rice

In a shallow bowl, combine shrimp, wine, salt, and pepper; set aside for 20 minutes. In a large skillet, heat 4 tablespoons of the oil until very hot. Add shrimp; stir-fry just until opaque. Remove shrimp from skillet and set aside. Heat remaining oil. Add garlic and ginger; stir-fry 10 seconds. Add green onions and black beans; stir-fry 15 seconds. Add pork and green pepper; stir-fry until cooked, about 3 minutes. In a separate bowl, stir together cornstarch and soy sauce until smooth. Blend in chicken stock and sesame oil. Add mixture to skillet; cook until sauce is slightly thickened. Add shrimp; cook until heated through. Add eggs, without stirring; cook, covered, for 1 minute, then stir to combine. Serve with hot rice.

LOBSTER AND PEA POD STIR-FRY

Makes 6 servings

  2 teaspoons cornstarch
½ teaspoon sugar
½ teaspoon salt
  1 teaspoon soy sauce
½ cup chicken broth
  1 tablespoon peanut oil
  1 clove garlic
  2 pounds lobster, shelled and cut into 1-inch pieces
½ cup sliced mushrooms
½ cup diced celery
½ cup diced bamboo shoots
½ cup diced water chestnuts
½ pound Chinese pea pods
¾ cup cashew nuts

Mix cornstarch with sugar, salt, soy sauce, and broth; set aside. In a wok or skillet over high heat, sauté garlic in peanut oil until brown. Remove garlic from wok. Add lobster and mushrooms; stir-fry 30 seconds. Add celery, bamboo shoots, water chestnuts, and pea pods; stir-fry 30 seconds. Stir cornstarch mixture and combine with vegetable mixture. Simmer, stirring constantly until sauce thickens. Stir in cashews.

ORIENTAL SHRIMP BALLS

Makes 6 servings

  1 pound shrimp, shelled, deveined, and pureed
½ teaspoon salt
½ teaspoon ground ginger
  2 tablespoons cornstarch
  1 egg white, lightly beaten
  2 cups peanut oil
    Sweet and sour sauce

In a large mixing bowl, combine pureed shrimp, salt, ginger, and cornstarch. Slowly add egg white. Dust hands with cornstarch. Roll shrimp mixture into 1-inch balls. In a deep saucepan, heat oil to 375°. Fry shrimp balls, a few at a time, until browned. Drain on paper towels. Serve with sweet and sour sauce.

BLACKENED FRIED REDFISH

Makes 6 servings

½ pound butter
  4 tablespoons lemon or lime juice
    Salt and pepper to taste
    Dash cayenne pepper
  1 teaspoon thyme
2¼ pounds redfish or other fillets (such as red snapper or bluefish)

In a medium saucepan over medium heat, melt butter. Stir in lemon juice and seasonings. Pour seasoned butter into a shallow bowl. Heat a large cast-iron skillet over high heat. Dip fillets into seasoned butter and fry quickly, turning once. The fillets will be charred on the outside. Transfer to a warmed platter. Add remaining seasoned butter to skillet, stirring to loosen browned bits on the bottom. Drizzle butter over fish.

Lobster and Pea Pod Stir-Fry

DEEP-FRIED SHRIMP

Makes 6 servings

½ cup all-purpose flour
½ teaspoon baking powder
　Salt and pepper to taste
　Dash garlic powder
2 tablespoons minced fresh parsley
1 egg, lightly beaten
⅓ cup milk
3 cups vegetable oil
1½ pounds large shrimp, shelled and deveined

In a medium bowl, combine flour, baking powder, seasonings, and parsley; mix well. Stir in egg and milk; mix until smooth. Set batter aside for 20 minutes. In a deep skillet, heat oil to 375°. Dip shrimp into batter and fry, a few at a time, until golden brown. Drain on paper towels.

SHRIMP WITH BROCCOLI

Makes 4 servings

¾ pound cooked shrimp, shelled and deveined
1 tablespoon dry sherry
2 tablespoons peanut oil
3 green onions, chopped
1 teaspoon minced gingerroot
1 pound broccoli, blanched and cut into 1-inch pieces
¼ cup chicken broth
　Salt to taste
2 teaspoons cornstarch mixed with 1 tablespoon cold water
½ teaspoon sesame oil
2 cups cooked rice

Sprinkle shrimp with sherry; set aside to marinate for 1 hour. In a wok or large skillet, heat oil over high heat. Add green onions and gingerroot; stir-fry for 30 seconds. Add broccoli; stir-fry for 10 seconds. Add shrimp, chicken broth, and salt. Bring to a simmer. Stir in cornstarch mixture. Heat and stir until thickened. Stir in sesame oil. Serve over hot cooked rice.

SALMON PATTIES

Makes 5 or 6 servings

1 15½-ounce can salmon, drained and broken into chunks; bones removed
1 medium onion, chopped
½ cup dry bread crumbs
2 eggs, beaten
　Salt and pepper to taste
3 tablespoons butter
3 tablespoons vegetable oil
　Parsley sprigs

In a deep bowl, combine all ingredients except butter, oil, and parsley. Form mixture into patties. In a large skillet, heat butter and vegetable oil until mixture sizzles. Add patties; fry on both sides until golden brown, turning once. Drain on paper towels. Garnish with parsley sprigs.

FRIED FISH WITH BEVERLY'S BARBECUE SAUCE

Makes 4 servings

2 pounds swordfish, cut into
  serving-sized pieces
  Salt and pepper to taste
½ cup cornstarch
4 tablespoons peanut oil
3 ribs celery, sliced
2 cups sliced mushrooms
½ teaspoon tarragon
  Beverly's Barbecue Sauce

Sprinkle swordfish with salt and pepper. Roll fish in cornstarch; shake gently to remove excess. In a heavy skillet over medium-high heat, fry fish quickly in peanut oil, turning once. Transfer fish to a heated platter. Reheat oil. Add celery and mushrooms; sprinkle with tarragon. Sauté until vegetables are tender. Arrange vegetables on platter around fish. Serve with Beverly's Barbecue Sauce.

BEVERLY'S BARBECUE SAUCE

1 cup catsup
¼ cup water
¼ cup butter
3 tablespoons vinegar
3 tablespoons orange juice
3 tablespoons lemon juice
3 tablespoons sugar
1 teaspoon Worcestershire sauce
1 medium onion, chopped
¼ teaspoon Tabasco sauce
  Salt, pepper, and garlic salt
  to taste

In a small saucepan over medium-low heat, combine all ingredients. Simmer for 10 minutes.

GINGERED TURBOT WITH MUSHROOMS

Makes 6 servings

3 tablespoons butter
2 tablespoons peanut oil
2 cloves garlic, minced
1 tablespoon minced fresh ginger
½ pound sliced mushrooms
2¼ pounds turbot fillets, cut into
  serving-sized pieces

In a large heavy skillet over medium heat, melt butter with oil until mixture sizzles. Add garlic and ginger; sauté until tender. Add mushrooms; sauté until tender. Push mushrooms over to one side of skillet or transfer to a plate. Reheat oil and butter, adding more butter if needed; sauté fish until tender, turning once. Return mushrooms to skillet and heat. Serve fish on a heated platter surrounded by sautéd mushrooms.

FRIED MISSISSIPPI CATFISH

Makes 6 servings

All-purpose flour
Salt and pepper to taste
2 pounds catfish fillets
2 eggs, lightly beaten
½ cup peanut oil
5 tablespoons butter
1 tablespoon lime juice
1 tablespoon chopped fresh dill

Season flour with salt and pepper. Roll fillets in seasoned flour, dip in eggs, and roll in flour again. In a large skillet, heat oil to 375°. Add fish; sauté until golden brown, turning once (about 8 minutes). Transfer to a warmed serving platter. In a small saucepan over medium heat, melt butter. Stir in lime juice and dill. Drizzle flavored butter over fried fish.

ILLINOIS SMELTS

Makes 4 servings

2 pounds fresh smelts, heads removed
½ cup milk
1 cup cornmeal
Salt and pepper to taste
½ cup butter

Wash fish and pat dry with paper towels. Dip smelts in milk, then cornmeal. Sprinkle with salt and pepper. In a large heavy skillet over medium heat, melt butter until it sizzles. Add smelts; fry, turning once, for about 4 minutes on each side.

FRIED SQUID

Makes 6 servings

2 cups vegetable oil
2 pounds squid, cleaned and cut into ½-inch rounds
All-purpose flour
½ teaspoon salt
2 lemons, cut into wedges

In a deep saucepan or skillet, heat oil to 375°. Toss squid in flour, shaking off excess so that just a light coating remains. Slide squid into hot oil a few pieces at a time; fry for 3 to 4 minutes or until cooked; drain on paper towels. Sprinkle with salt and garnish with lemon wedges.

IPSWICH FRIED CLAMS

Makes 4 servings

3 to 4 dozen shelled clams
All-purpose flour
Salt and pepper to taste
2 eggs, lightly beaten
1 cup bread crumbs
2 cups peanut oil
Tartar sauce

Wash clams and pat dry with paper towels. Roll clams in flour; season with salt and pepper. Dip clams in eggs and roll in bread crumbs. In a deep saucepan, heat oil to 375°. Fry clams, a few at a time, until golden brown. Remove from oil with a slotted spoon and drain on paper towels. Serve with tartar sauce.

Red Snapper Veracruz, page 44

BAKED

RED SNAPPER VERACRUZ

Makes 8 servings

3 pounds red snapper, cut into
  2-inch pieces
4 tablespoons lime juice
1 teaspoon salt
¼ cup olive oil
1 clove garlic, minced
1 large onion, sliced
2 pounds tomatoes, peeled and
  chopped
2 medium green peppers, cut
  into strips
4 large potatoes, peeled, sliced,
  and half-cooked
4 bay leaves
½ teaspoon oregano
½ cup sliced green olives
  Lemon slices

Arrange fish in an ovenproof serving dish; sprinkle with lime juice and salt. Refrigerate, covered, for 2 hours. Preheat oven to 325°. In a medium skillet, heat oil. Add garlic and onion; sauté until onion is tender. Add tomatoes, green peppers, potatoes, bay leaves, and oregano; simmer 10 minutes. Cover fish pieces with tomato mixture. Bake for 35 minutes or until fish flakes easily when tested with a fork. Remove bay leaves. Sprinkle with olives; garnish with lemon slices.

DIETER'S FISH DELIGHT

Makes 4 servings

3 ribs celery, sliced
2 medium zucchini, sliced in
  ¼-inch rounds
½ pound mushrooms, sliced
¾ cup spicy tomato juice
1 teaspoon Worcestershire sauce
1½ pounds fillet of flounder
  Salt and pepper to taste

Preheat oven to 400°. In a small saucepan over medium heat, combine all ingredients except fish, salt, and pepper. Simmer for 4 minutes, stirring occasionally. Place fish in a shallow casserole. Season with salt and pepper. Spoon vegetable mixture over fish. Bake, uncovered, for 8 minutes or until fish flakes easily when tested with a fork.

BAKED SEA BASS WITH LIME JUICE

Makes 6 servings

2 pounds sea bass fillets
½ teaspoon garlic powder
  Salt and pepper to taste
3 tablespoons butter
3 tablespoons olive oil
3 tablespoons lime juice

Preheat oven to 350°. Sprinkle fillets with garlic powder, salt, and pepper. In a large heavy skillet over medium heat, melt butter with olive oil until hot. Add fish; baste with olive oil and bake for 20 minutes or until fish flakes easily when tested with a fork. Baste twice during cooking. Transfer fish to a heated serving platter. Drizzle with lime juice.

44

BAKED STUFFED CRAB

Makes 6 servings

5 tablespoons butter
1 large onion, chopped
1 6½-ounce can crab meat
   (remove gristle)
½ cup heavy cream
2 tablespoons chopped fresh
   parsley
3 dashes Tabasco sauce
¼ teaspoon thyme
   Salt to taste
¾ cup bread crumbs
2 tablespoons butter

Preheat oven to 400°. In a large skillet over medium heat, melt butter. Add onion; sauté until tender. Remove skillet from heat and add remaining ingredients, except bread crumbs and 2 tablespoons butter. Cook mixture over medium heat for 2 minutes. Mix in ½ cup bread crumbs. Spoon mixture lightly into custard cups or crab shells. Sprinkle with remaining bread crumbs; dot with butter. Place custard cups on a baking sheet; bake for 5 minutes.

BAKED STUFFED SHRIMP

Makes 6 servings

24 jumbo shrimp, shelled and
   deveined (leave tails attached)
2 cups cracker crumbs
½ cup melted butter
¼ cup chopped fresh parsley
½ teaspoon garlic powder
   Black pepper to taste

Preheat oven to 400°. Butterfly shrimp by cutting along inside curve, almost to the vein. Open and flatten to form the butterfly shape. In a small bowl, toss cracker crumbs with butter; stir in parsley, garlic powder, and pepper. Place butterflied shrimp on a baking sheet, cut side down. On the center of each shrimp, place 1 tablespoon of the crumb mixture. Bake for 10 minutes.

CAPE COD STUFFED CLAMS

Makes 4 servings

4 tablespoons butter
1 small onion, chopped
3 tablespoons all-purpose flour
4 egg yolks, lightly beaten
2 6½-ounce cans minced clams,
   drained (reserve liquid)
1 tablespoon chopped fresh
   parsley
   Salt and pepper to taste
1 cup buttered bread crumbs

Preheat oven to 375°. In a medium saucepan over low heat, melt butter. Add onion; cook until tender. Whisk in flour; cook until well blended. Gradually stir in egg yolks, blending thoroughly until smooth. Stir in clams, parsley, and enough reserved clam liquid to make a sauce. Season with salt and pepper. Spoon clam mixture into 16 clam shells or 4 custard cups. Sprinkle with buttered bread crumbs. Place clam shells or custard cups in a shallow pan. Pour hot water into the pan to a depth of 1 inch. Bake for 20 minutes.

TROUT WITH SPINACH AND MUSHROOM STUFFING

Makes 6 servings

5 tablespoons butter
2 cloves garlic, minced
1 small onion, finely chopped
1 cup chopped mushrooms
1 10-ounce package frozen chopped spinach, thawed and squeezed dry
1 cup bread crumbs
½ teaspoon tarragon
¼ teaspoon thyme
  Salt and pepper to taste
1 whole trout (about 3½ pounds), cleaned (leave head and tail attached)

Preheat oven to 350°. Grease a baking sheet. In a large skillet over medium heat, melt 3 tablespoons of the butter. Add garlic, onion, and mushrooms; sauté for 2 minutes. Add spinach; sauté for 1 minute. Stir in bread crumbs and seasonings; cook for 2 minutes. Place trout on prepared baking sheet. Spoon stuffing into cavity. Dot fish with remaining butter. Bake, uncovered, for 40 minutes or until fish flakes easily when tested with a fork. Let stand 5 minutes before serving.

SHRIMP DE JONGHE

Makes 6 servings

6 tablespoons butter, melted
½ cup dry sherry
¼ cup chopped fresh parsley
3 cloves garlic, minced
¼ teaspoon cayenne pepper
2 cups fine bread crumbs
2 pounds medium shrimp, cooked, shelled, and deveined (leave tails attached)

Preheat oven to 325°. In a large mixing bowl, stir together butter, sherry, parsley, garlic, and cayenne. Stir in bread crumbs. Arrange shrimp in a shallow ovenproof casserole; sprinkle with bread crumb mixture. Bake for 10 minutes. Serve from the casserole or in individual seafood shells.

BAKED MACKEREL

Makes 6 servings

1 fresh mackerel (about 3½ pounds), split, backbone removed, skin intact
3 strips bacon, cut in half
3 tomatoes, cut in half
½ cup seasoned bread crumbs
2 tablespoons butter, cut into 6 pieces
  Lemon wedges

Preheat oven to 350°. Pat fish dry with paper towels. Place on a broiler rack, skin side down. Cross bacon strips over mackerel. Arrange tomato halves around fish; sprinkle with bread crumbs and dot with a piece of butter. Bake for 15 minutes or until fish flakes easily when tested with a fork. Transfer fish to a warmed serving platter. Surround with tomatoes and garnish with lemon wedges.

Trout with Spinach and Mushroom Stuffing

INDIVIDUAL STUFFED FISH

Makes 6 servings

2 tomatoes, peeled and sliced
6 tablespoons bread crumbs
½ teaspoon tarragon
Salt and pepper to taste
6 whole red snappers
(about 1 pound each)
½ cup dry white wine
6 tablespoons butter
2 teaspoons lime juice
4 tablespoons grated Parmesan cheese
Parsley sprigs

Preheat oven to 500°. Arrange tomato slices in 2 baking pans; sprinkle with bread crumbs and season with tarragon, salt, and pepper. Place whole fishes on bread crumbs. In a small saucepan over low heat, combine wine, butter, and lime juice. Cook, stirring often, until butter melts; drizzle over fish. Sprinkle fish with Parmesan cheese; bake for 15 minutes or until fish flakes easily when tested with a fork. Garnish each serving with parsley sprigs.

FINNAN HADDIE

Makes 6 servings

2½ pounds smoked haddock, cut into 1-inch pieces
2 cups milk
1 cup sour cream
1 cup heavy cream
1 tablespoon minced dill
Toast points

In a glass bowl, soak haddock pieces in milk for 4 to 6 hours. Place fish and milk in a glass or ceramic baking pan; bake for 15 minutes at 400°. Remove pan from oven. With a slotted spoon, transfer fish to a serving platter. In a small saucepan, combine 1 cup of the pan juices with sour cream, heavy cream, and dill. Cook over medium heat until warm. Stir in fish; cook until heated through. Serve over toast points.

POMPANO IN PAPER

Makes 6 servings

3 tablespoons butter
1 small onion, chopped
¾ cup sliced mushrooms
1 red bell pepper, cut into strips
6 6-ounce pompano fillets
6 ounces red wine
1 cup water
½ teaspoon Worcestershire sauce
½ teaspoon salt
Parchment paper

Preheat oven to 350°. In a heavy skillet over medium heat, melt butter. Add onion, mushrooms, and red pepper; sauté until vegetables are tender. Arrange fillets over vegetables. Add wine, water, Worcestershire sauce, and salt; simmer for 5 minutes. Remove from heat. From parchment paper, cut 6 hearts, each longer than a fillet. Oil the parchment. Place a fillet on one side of each heart; top with vegetable mixture. Fold hearts over fillets sealing edges together. Place filled hearts, sealed edges down, on a baking sheet. Bake until packets puff, about 10 minutes. Slit open packets and serve.

BAKED SOLE WITH MUSHROOMS AND SOUR CREAM

Makes 8 servings

4 large cooked potatoes, thinly sliced
¾ pound mushrooms, sliced
4 tablespoons butter, cut into small pieces
½ teaspoon tarragon
½ teaspoon salt
¾ cup dry white wine
1½ cups sour cream
2¼ pounds fillet of sole, cut into serving-sized pieces

Preheat oven to 325°. Arrange sliced potatoes in the bottom of an 11 x 7-inch baking dish. Scatter mushrooms over potatoes and dot with butter. Season with tarragon and salt. Drizzle wine over mushrooms. Top with half of the sour cream. Arrange fish pieces over sour cream; spread with remaining sour cream. Bake for 25 to 30 minutes.

BAKED FISH WITH ORANGE AND LIME

Makes 6 servings

½ cup bread crumbs
½ teaspoon thyme
Salt and pepper to taste
¼ cup orange juice
2 pounds fillet of sole, cut into serving-sized pieces
¼ cup Curacao liqueur
1 clove garlic, minced
1 teaspoon grated orange peel
Lime wedges

Grease a large, shallow casserole. In a shallow bowl, combine bread crumbs, thyme, salt, and pepper; stir in orange juice. Bread each piece of fillet, on one side only, with the crumb mixture. Place in prepared casserole; chill for 1 hour. Preheat oven to 375°. Bake fish for 10 minutes. Combine liqueur, garlic, and orange peel; drizzle over fish. Bake for 15 minutes more, basting fish with accumulated liquid. Garnish with lime wedges.

BAKED HALIBUT STEAKS WITH ORANGE-TOMATO SAUCE

Makes 6 servings

2 teaspoons grated orange peel
½ cup boiling water
2 large tomatoes, peeled and chopped
1 clove garlic, minced
½ teaspoon marjoram
6 halibut steaks, ¾-inch thick

Preheat oven to 350°. In a small mixing bowl, cover orange peel with boiling water. Let stand for 1 minute; drain. Add tomatoes, garlic, and marjoram. Cut 6 pieces of aluminum foil, each twice the size of a halibut steak. Place one piece of fish in the center of each piece of aluminum foil. Spoon 2 tablespoons of the tomato mixture over each steak. Fold aluminum foil around fish, envelope-style. Place wrapped fish on a baking sheet. Bake for 20 minutes. Serve fish in packets to be opened at the table.

BAKED WHOLE WHITEFISH WITH TOMATOES AND WATERCRESS SAUCE

Makes 6 servings

1 large onion, thinly sliced
5 ribs celery, thinly sliced
1 whole whitefish (about 3½ pounds), scaled, head and tail removed
½ teaspoon chervil
Salt and pepper to taste
1 16-ounce can tomatoes, cut into pieces, with juice
Watercress Sauce

Preheat oven to 400°. Line the bottom of a large baking dish with a bed of sliced onions and celery. Place whitefish over vegetables. Season with chervil, salt, and pepper. Distribute tomatoes and juice over fish. Bake for 45 minutes or until fish flakes easily when tested with a fork. Transfer fish carefully to a serving platter. Serve with Watercress Sauce.

WATERCRESS SAUCE

Makes 1½ cups sauce

1 small onion, minced
½ cup watercress, stems removed
¾ cup mayonnaise
¾ cup sour cream
Salt and pepper to taste

In a blender or food processor, combine all ingredients; blend until smooth. Refrigerate in a covered container until ready to serve.

BAKED WHOLE SEA BASS

Makes 6 servings

1 whole sea bass (about 3½ pounds), split
Lemon juice
Salt and pepper to taste
4 sprigs celery leaves
1 small onion, sliced
2 tablespoons butter
2 tablespoons olive oil
1 medium onion, chopped
3 ribs celery, sliced
½ pound mushrooms, sliced
1 cup dry white wine
Lemon wedges

Preheat oven to 350°. Oil a baking dish. Wash the fish and pat dry with paper towels. Rub inside and outside with lemon juice, salt, and pepper. Arrange celery leaves and onion slices in the fish cavity. Arrange remaining onion slices on the bottom of the oiled baking dish. Place fish on top of onion slices. In a medium skillet over medium heat, melt butter with oil. Add chopped onion and celery; sauté until tender. Add mushrooms; sauté until tender. Spoon vegetables over fish. Drizzle wine over all. Bake, uncovered, for 20 minutes or until fish flakes easily when tested with a fork. Baste with more melted butter and wine during cooking if fish looks dry. Serve fish on a heated platter. Garnish with lemon wedges.

Flounder-Salmon Rolls in Lobster Sauce, page 52

STEAMED AND POACHED

FLOUNDER-SALMON ROLLS IN LOBSTER SAUCE

Makes 8 servings

1 salmon steak (about 1 pound), skinned and boned
4 flounder *or* sole fillets (about 8 ounces each)
2 teaspoons lemon juice
¼ teaspoon pepper
½ cup water
½ cup dry white wine
2 shallots, thinly sliced
½ teaspoon salt
1 tarragon leaf
1½ cups heavy cream
1 6½-ounce can lobster meat, drained, boned, and coarsely shredded
¼ teaspoon salt
⅛ teaspoon paprika

Cut salmon steak in half crosswise; cut each half into 4 strips. Cut each flounder fillet in half lengthwise; sprinkle with lemon juice and pepper. Place a strip of salmon on each fillet; roll fillet around salmon and secure with wooden picks. In a large skillet, combine water, wine, shallots, and salt. Tie tarragon leaf in a piece of cheesecloth; add to skillet. Stand fish rolls in skillet. Over medium-high heat, bring liquid in skillet to a boil. Lower heat; simmer, covered, for 5 minutes or until fish is white and firm. Transfer fish rolls to a platter and keep warm. Cook liquid rapidly until reduced to ½ cup; remove tarragon; set liquid aside. In a large saucepan over medium-high heat, cook cream, stirring constantly, until reduced to 1 cup. Stir in reserved fish liquid, lobster meat, salt, and paprika; cook and stir until hot. Pour sauce over flounder-salmon rolls.

BOILED LOBSTER

Makes 6 servings

1 tablespoon salt
6 live lobsters (1½ pounds each)
¼ pound butter, melted
2 lemons, cut into wedges
¼ cup chopped parsley

Fill a large kettle or stock pot with water and bring to a rapid boil. Add salt. Plunge lobsters, heads first, into the water. Cover pot and boil lobsters 6 to 8 minutes; lobsters will turn bright red. Remove lobsters with tongs. Slit the underside of each lobster with a sharp knife. Remove the stomach, lungs, and intestinal vein. Serve lobster with melted butter; garnish with lemon wedges and parsley.

STEAMED MUSSELS IN WHITE WINE AND CREAM

Makes 4 servings

48 large mussels, scrubbed
   and debearded
2 green onions, finely chopped
1 cup dry white wine
1 cup heavy cream
1 cup carrots, cut into julienne
   strips
1 cup sliced leeks
1 cup Hollandaise Sauce
2 to 3 tablespoons chopped fresh
   parsley

In a large covered saucepan over medium heat, steam mussels and green onions in wine until mussels open. Discard any unopened mussels. Remove pan from heat and drain liquid into a skillet set on medium heat. Stir in cream and vegetables; simmer until liquid is reduced by half. Stir in Hollandaise Sauce; blend well. Place 12 mussels in each of 4 serving dishes. Top with sauce and sprinkle with parsley.

HOLLANDAISE SAUCE

Makes ¾ cup

4 egg yolks, lightly beaten
  Salt and white pepper to taste
1 tablespoon lemon juice
¼ pound butter at room
   temperature

In the top of a double boiler over warm, not boiling, water, combine egg yolks, salt, pepper, and lemon juice. Beat mixture until it begins to thicken, about 10 minutes. Beat in butter, 1 tablespoon at a time, until well blended.

FISH PROVENCALE

Makes 6 servings

1¾ pounds flounder or haddock
    fillets
    Salt and paprika to taste
1 tablespoon butter
1 medium onion, thinly sliced
2 cloves garlic, minced
½ cup dry white wine
½ pound mushrooms, sliced
3 sprigs parsley, minced
1 vegetable bouillon cube
2 tomatoes, peeled or 1
   16-ounce can tomatoes,
   drained
1 teaspoon honey
1 tablespoon cornstarch dissolved
   in ½ cup cold water

Sprinkle each fillet with salt and paprika. In a large skillet over medium heat, melt butter. Add onion and garlic; sauté until tender. Add wine, mushrooms, parsley, vegetable bouillon cube, tomatoes, and honey. Bring mixture to a simmer. Arrange fish on top of vegetables. Cover and simmer 15 to 20 minutes or until fish flakes easily when tested with a fork. With a slotted spoon, carefully transfer fish to a heated serving dish; keep warm. Stir cornstarch mixture; add to skillet. Cook, stirring constantly, until sauce thickens. Ladle sauce over fish.

WISCONSIN FISH BOIL

Makes 8 servings

½ pound salt
1 pound small red potatoes
3½ pounds fish steaks (whitefish, salmon, *or* trout), cut into 1-inch cross sections
Parsley for garnish
¼ pound butter, melted

In a stockpot, bring 2 gallons of water to a boil. Stir in ¼ pound of the salt. Place potatoes in a wire basket; immerse in water and boil gently for 15 minutes. Remove potatoes; transfer to a heated platter. Add remaining salt to boiling water. Place fish in a wire basket; plunge into boiling water. Cook 6 to 7 minutes or until fish flakes easily when tested with a fork. Transfer to platter with potatoes. Garnish with parsley. Serve with plenty of melted butter. Round out the traditional Wisconsin menu with coleslaw, rye bread, and cherry pie.

SWORDFISH WITH PASTA

Makes 6 servings

1 pound fine pasta
1½ pounds swordfish, cut into strips
¾ pound bay scallops
3 tablespoons butter
2 large leeks, cut into rounds and separated
3 tomatoes, peeled and chopped
½ teaspoon thyme
Salt and pepper to taste

Cook pasta according to package directions; drain and set aside. Steam swordfish and scallops until fish flakes easily when tested with a fork, about 5 minutes. While fish steams, melt butter; add leeks and sauté until tender. Add tomatoes and cooked pasta; toss to mix. Season with thyme, salt, and pepper. Divide pasta among 6 plates. Serve steamed fish and scallops over pasta.

POACHED FISH FILLETS

Makes 4 servings

4 fresh *or* thawed frozen fish fillets, such as flounder, sole, cod, *or* haddock (about 1½ pounds)
½ cup dry white wine
¼ cup water
4 thin lemon slices
Leaves from 2 ribs celery
1 bay leaf
½ teaspoon seasoned salt
⅛ teaspoon white pepper
Paprika
Tartar sauce

Preheat oven to 350°. Arrange fish in a buttered baking dish. Combine wine and water; pour over fish. Arrange lemon slices on fillets; add celery leaves, bay leaf, salt, and pepper. Cover baking dish. Poach fish in oven for about 12 minutes or until fish flakes easily when tested with a fork. Before serving, sprinkle fillets lightly with paprika. Use a slotted spoon to remove fish from liquid. Serve with tartar sauce.

Poached Fish Fillets

SCALLOPS IN PUFF PASTRY

Makes 6 servings

4 tablespoons butter
2 tablespoons peanut oil
1 onion, thinly sliced
1 carrot, cut into thin strips
1 zucchini, thinly sliced
1½ pounds bay scallops
½ cup heavy cream
1 teaspoon chervil
6 tablespoons butter, cut into pieces
6 puff pastry shells, baked according to package directions
3 tablespoons minced parsley

In a large skillet, heat butter and oil. Add vegetables; sauté until tender. Remove vegetables from skillet and set aside. Steam scallops over hot water until opaque; drain. Reheat butter remaining in skillet. Stir in cream and chervil. Whisk in butter, one piece at a time, until mixture is smooth. Place drained scallops in puff pastry; arrange reserved vegetables around pastry. Drizzle sauce over all. Sprinkle with parsley.

ALMOND SOLE

Makes 6 servings

1 large onion, thinly sliced
½ pound mushrooms, chopped
2 pounds fillet of sole, about ¾-inch thick
½ teaspoon rosemary
½ teaspoon salt
½ cup sherry
1½ cups half-and-half
2 tablespoons butter
¾ cup toasted almonds

Place onions and mushrooms in a large skillet. Arrange fish over vegetables; sprinkle with rosemary and salt. Pour sherry over all. Simmer, covered, over low heat for 10 minutes. Transfer fish to a shallow casserole. Simmer vegetables in remaining liquid, over high heat, until liquid is reduced by half. Lower heat; stir in half-and-half and butter. Return mixture to a boil. Pour mixture over fish, distributing onions and mushrooms evenly. Sprinkle almonds over top. Broil about 4 inches from heat for 2 minutes or until fish flakes easily when tested with a fork.

SIMPLY MUSSELS

Makes 6 servings

3 tablespoons butter
4 sprigs celery leaves
4 sprigs parsley
1 onion, thinly sliced
3 pounds mussels, scrubbed and debearded
1 cup dry white wine
½ teaspoon pepper

In a large saucepan over medium heat, melt butter. Add celery leaves, parsley, and onion; sauté until tender. Add mussels, wine, and pepper; cover pan tightly. Simmer for about 8 minutes or until the mussels open. Discard any unopened mussels. Strain broth. Transfer mussels and broth to a deep serving bowl. Serve with crusty bread.

CASSEROLES

FISH AND CHEESE ASPARAGUS CASSEROLE

Makes 3 to 4 servings

1 pound fish steaks *or* fillets, cut
  into serving-sized pieces
¼ teaspoon dill
  Salt and pepper to taste
1 10-ounce package frozen cut
  asparagus
1 10½-ounce can Cheddar
  cheese soup
¼ cup milk
1 cup soft bread crumbs
2 tablespoons melted butter

Preheat oven to 325°. Arrange fish pieces in a greased baking dish; sprinkle with dill, salt, and pepper. Bake, uncovered, for 35 minutes. While fish bakes, cook asparagus according to package directions; drain and place on top of fish. In a small bowl, stir together soup and milk until well mixed; pour over fish. Stir together bread crumbs and melted butter; sprinkle over soup. Return casserole to oven; bake until crumbs are lightly browned.

CRAB MEAT CASSEROLE

Makes 6 servings

3 eggs, well beaten
2 cups ricotta cheese
1 tablespoon cornstarch
2 7½-ounce cans crab meat
  (remove gristle)
1 red onion, thinly sliced
  Salt to taste
½ teaspoon basil
½ cup seasoned bread crumbs

Preheat oven to 350°. Grease a 2½-quart casserole. Stir together eggs and cheese until well mixed. Add remaining ingredients, except bread crumbs; mix well. Spoon mixture into prepared casserole; place in a baking pan. Pour hot water into the baking pan to a depth of 1 inch. Sprinkle casserole with seasoned bread crumbs. Bake for 25 minutes or until the casserole is set.

TUNA TETTRAZZINI

Makes 6 servings

4 tablespoons butter
1 pound mushrooms, sliced
4 tablespoons all-purpose flour
2½ cups half-and-half
¼ cup sherry
1 8-ounce package processed
  American cheese, grated
  Salt and pepper to taste
½ pound thin spaghetti, cooked
  and drained
3 6½-ounce cans tuna, drained
  and flaked
4 tablespoons grated Parmesan
  cheese

Preheat oven to 350°. In a large skillet over medium heat, melt butter. Add mushrooms; sauté until tender. Stir in flour until well blended. Stir in half-and-half; cook, stirring constantly, until mixture thickens. Stir in sherry, cheese, salt, and pepper. Cook, stirring constantly, until cheese melts. In a large mixing bowl, toss together spaghetti, cheese sauce, and tuna. Spoon into a 2-quart shallow baking dish; sprinkle with Parmesan cheese. Bake for 15 minutes.

EASY SALMON-NOODLE CASSEROLE

Makes 6 servings

½ pound wide egg noodles, cooked and drained
2 tablespoons butter, melted
1½ cups sour cream
½ teaspoon tarragon
½ teaspoon salt
1½ cups sliced mushrooms
1 15½-ounce can salmon, drained and boned
½ cup seasoned bread crumbs

Preheat oven to 350°. Grease a 3-quart casserole. Toss noodles with melted butter. Stir in sour cream. Add remaining ingredients, except bread crumbs; toss until well mixed. Pour noodle mixture into prepared casserole. Sprinkle with bread crumbs. Bake for 15 to 20 minutes or until crumbs are lightly browned.

PARTY CRAB MEAT CASSEROLE

Makes 6 servings

¼ cup butter
½ pound mushrooms, thinly sliced
1 green pepper, cut into strips
½ cup diced celery
½ cup thinly sliced green onions
2 10¾-ounce cans condensed cream of celery soup
¼ cup lemon juice
⅛ teaspoon hot pepper sauce
½ teaspoon celery salt
½ teaspoon salt
2 6-ounce packages frozen crab meat, thawed, drained, and flaked
6 frozen patty shells, baked according to package directions

In a large skillet, melt butter. Add mushrooms, green pepper, celery, and onions; cook, stirring often, until vegetables are tender (about 5 minutes). Stir in soup, lemon juice, hot pepper sauce, and seasonings; cook until hot. Stir in crab meat; heat through. Serve in patty shells.

HOT CRAB MEAT CASSEROLE

Makes 4 servings

½ pound flaked, cooked crab meat
2 3-ounce packages cream cheese
2 teaspoons horseradish
3 tablespoons heavy cream
½ small onion, chopped
¼ teaspoon cayenne
2 English muffins, split

Preheat oven to 350°. In a food processor, blend all ingredients, except muffins, until smooth. Spoon into a 1-quart casserole and bake for 15 minutes. Serve on toasted English muffins.

Party Crab Meat Casserole

SALMON MACARONI BAKE

Makes 6 servings

4 tablespoons butter
1 small onion, chopped
2 ribs celery, sliced
4 tablespoons all-purpose flour
1 teaspoon dry mustard
2½ cups milk
1 teaspoon Worcestershire sauce
2 cups grated Cheddar cheese
1 15½-ounce can salmon, drained, boned, and flaked
½ pound macaroni, cooked and drained

Preheat oven to 350°. Grease a 3-quart baking dish. In a large saucepan over medium heat, melt butter. Add onion and celery; sauté until vegetables are tender, stirring often. Stir in flour and mustard until well blended. Stir in milk and Worcestershire sauce; cook, stirring constantly, until mixture thickens. Add 1½ cups of the cheese; stir until cheese melts. Stir salmon and macaroni into cheese sauce. Spoon into prepared baking dish. Sprinkle with remaining cheese. Bake 30 minutes.

SCALLOP MOUSSE

Makes 6 to 8 servings

1¾ pounds scallops
¼ cup all-purpose flour
1 teaspoon salt
½ teaspoon white pepper
½ teaspoon ground nutmeg
4 eggs, beaten
1½ cups heavy cream

Preheat oven to 350°. Grease a 2-quart casserole. In a food processor, puree scallops; transfer to a mixing bowl. Add flour, salt, pepper, and nutmeg; blend well. Stir in eggs and heavy cream; mix until blended. Spoon mixture into prepared casserole; place in a larger baking pan. Pour hot water into the baking pan to a depth of at least 1 inch. Bake, uncovered, for 1 hour or until a knife inserted near the center comes out clean. Serve directly from casserole, warm or cold.

SCALLOPED FISH

Makes 8 servings

4 tablespoons butter
4 tablespoons all-purpose flour
2 cups milk
½ teaspoon sage
½ teaspoon salt
3 cups flaked, cooked haddock or halibut
1½ cups diced, cooked potatoes
1½ cups seasoned bread crumbs
1 tablespoon butter

Preheat oven to 400°. Grease a 2-quart casserole. In a small saucepan over medium heat, melt butter. Stir in flour until well blended. Add milk; cook and stir until sauce thickens. Stir in sage and salt; remove from heat. In a bowl, toss fish and potatoes until mixed. Place half of the mixture in the prepared casserole; cover with half of the sauce. Repeat with remaining fish mixture and sauce. Sprinkle with bread crumbs and dot with butter. Bake for 30 minutes.

JAMBALAYA

Makes 8 to 10 servings

6 tablespoons butter
2 onions, thinly sliced
4 cloves garlic, minced
1 16-ounce can tomatoes
¼ cup tomato paste
2 ribs celery, thinly sliced
1 green pepper, cut into strips
2 tablespoons chopped parsley
½ teaspoon thyme
1 pound boiled ham, diced
2 pounds shrimp, cooked, shelled, and deveined
3 cups cooked rice
Salt, pepper, and cayenne to taste

Preheat oven to 350°. In a large skillet over medium heat, melt butter. Add onion and garlic; sauté until onion is tender. Add undrained tomatoes; break up with a spoon. Stir in tomato paste, celery, green pepper, parsley, and thyme until well mixed. Stir in ham, shrimp, and rice; season with salt, pepper, and cayenne. Spoon into a large casserole. Bake, covered, for 30 minutes.

SOUTHERN SCALLOPED OYSTERS

Makes 4 to 6 servings

2 cups cracker crumbs
½ teaspoon salt
¼ teaspoon white pepper
½ cup butter, melted
1 pint oysters, drained (reserve liquor)
¼ teaspoon Worcestershire sauce
1 cup cream

Preheat oven to 350°. Butter a 1-quart casserole. In a bowl, combine cracker crumbs, salt, pepper, and butter. Sprinkle ⅓ of the cracker mixture over the bottom of the prepared casserole; cover with a layer of oysters. Repeat layers, reserving ¼ cup of the cracker mixture for topping. Combine reserved oyster liquor and Worcestershire sauce with cream; pour over casserole. Top with remaining crumbs. Bake for 20 minutes or until topping begins to brown.

FISH LOAF

Makes 8 servings

2½ cups cooked firm-fleshed fish, pureed
1 medium onion, chopped
1 cup unflavored bread crumbs
2 cups half-and-half
3 eggs, lightly beaten
¼ cup chopped fresh parsley
½ teaspoon basil
½ teaspoon tarragon
Salt and pepper to taste
Sliced tomatoes

Preheat oven to 375°. Lightly oil a 9 x 5-inch loaf pan; fit bottom of pan with oiled waxed paper. In a mixing bowl, combine fish, onion, and bread crumbs. Stir in half-and-half, eggs, herbs, salt, and pepper. Pack mixture into prepared loaf pan; place in a larger baking pan. Pour hot water into baking pan to a depth of 2 inches. Bake for 45 minutes. Cool fish loaf completely. Unmold, discard waxed paper. Garnish with tomatoes.

SEAFOOD CREPES WITH MORNAY SAUCE

Makes 16 crepes

4 tablespoons butter *or* **margarine**
1 medium onion, chopped
½ pound mushrooms, sliced
2 cups cooked seafood: scallops, shrimp *or* **crab**
Mornay Sauce
½ cup grated Parmesan cheese
2 tablespoons chopped fresh parsley
½ teaspoon salt
¼ teaspoon white pepper
Luncheon Crepes
Paprika

Preheat oven to 375°. Grease a large, shallow baking dish. In a large skillet over medium heat, melt butter. Add onion and mushrooms; sauté until vegetables are tender. Stir in seafood. Blend in ¾ cup of Mornay Sauce, ¼ cup of Parmesan cheese, parsley, salt, and pepper. Spoon about 2 tablespoons of filling down the center of the unbrowned side of each crepe. Roll crepe and place seam side down in prepared baking dish. Repeat with remaining crepes. Pour remaining sauce over filled crepes and sprinkle with Parmesan cheese and paprika. Bake for 15 minutes.

MORNAY SAUCE

3 tablespoons butter *or* **margarine**
3 tablespoons all-purpose flour
2 cups milk
2 tablespoons dry white wine
2 tablespoons grated Swiss cheese
Salt and pepper to taste
1 egg yolk mixed with ½ cup half-and-half

In a small saucepan over medium heat, melt butter. Blend in flour. Stir in milk. Cook, stirring constantly, until sauce thickens. Add wine and cheese; blend well. Season with salt and pepper. Remove from heat. Add egg yolk mixture; blend well.

LUNCHEON CREPES

Makes 16 crepes

1 cup milk
½ cup water
2 eggs
2 tablespoons melted butter
2 tablespoons vegetable oil
1 cup all-purpose flour
¼ teaspoon salt

In a mixing bowl, combine all ingredients; blend until smooth. Cover batter; set aside at room temperature for 30 minutes. Butter or oil a crepe pan. Heat pan until butter sizzles or oil is hot. Add 2 tablespoons of the batter. Immediately tilt pan from side to side so that batter covers the bottom of the pan. Cook about 1½ minutes or until crepe is lightly browned on one side. Turn out onto a paper towel. Repeat with remaining batter.

Seafood Crepes with Mornay Sauce